S is for Silver

A Nevada Alphabet

Written by Eleanor Coerr and Illustrated by Darcie Park

Sleeping Bear Press

310 North Main Street, Suite 300
Chelsea, MI 48118
www.sleepingbearpress.com

THOMSON
™
GALE

© 2004 Thomson Gale, a part of the Thomson Corporation.

Thomson, Star Logo and Sleeping Bear Press are trademarks
and Gale is a registered trademark used herein under license.

Printed and bound in China.

10 9 8 7 6 5 4 3 2

Library of Congress Cataloging-in-Publication Data

Coerr, Eleanor.
S is for silver : a Nevada alphabet / written by Eleanor Coerr ;
illustrated by Darcie Park.
p. cm.
ISBN 1-58536-117-8
1. Nevada—Juvenile literature. 2. English language—Alphabet—Juvenile
literature. I. Park, Darcie, ill. II. Title.
F841.3.C64 2004
979.3—dc22   2004005957

For my grandchildren, Ethan and Warren

Special thanks to Amy
and other editors for their help.

ELEANOR

∾

Special thanks and love to my mom and dad, John and Nicole.
You've always been there for me. I don't know what
I would do without your love and inspiration.

To all my family, Tom, Bonnie, Sandy, Justin, Melia, and Nathan.
Your support and enthusiasm recharges me.

Thank you to my friends, Donna and Caryn,
for your help and friendship.

DARCIE

Our official state animal, the desert bighorn sheep can be found living in southern Nevada. Nevada's mountainous desert country is a good environment for the animal because it can survive without water for long periods. A male bighorn is about four and one-half feet tall and can weigh as much as 175 pounds.

There are two other kinds of bighorn sheep living in Nevada: California bighorn sheep in northwest Nevada, and Rocky Mountain bighorn sheep in northeast Nevada. In total there are nearly 1,500 of these proud animals left in our state, more than any other place in the world.

Aa

Animal is the word that begins with A
and one that's amazing in every way.
An awesome animal that is so great—
the bighorn sheep, animal of our state.

B is for mountain Bluebird,
our state bird we love to see
feeding their young, keeping them neat
and singing for us—oh so sweet.

In April of 1967 the mountain bluebird was named Nevada's state bird. In calm skies it can travel very fast—20 to 30 miles per hour. This bird is a brave survivor in our harsh desert climate.

A member of the thrush family, our bluebird's song is a clear, short warble. The bright blue-colored male doesn't have to sing for long to attract his more plain-colored mate. Female bluebirds are brownish gray with a white belly and undertail, and a bit of blue on their tail.

The female bluebird builds a cup-shaped nest using dry grass stems, plants, and thin strips of bark. It may take from two days to more than a week to finish building the nest. Once the nest is built, the female lays one egg each day until the clutch, usually with five or six eggs, is complete. Mountain bluebirds eat seeds, berries, fruit, and insects.

C

Carson City, that's our
where our capitol makes its home.
Here laws were made fair and right
under the silvery, shining dome.

When the Nevada Territory was
established in 1861, Carson City was
named as the territorial capital. After
Nevada was granted statehood in 1864
by Congress, Carson City became our
state capital.

A small spruce tree was planted in the
town square. In 1937 when the tree had
grown to 95 feet tall, it was adorned with
its first holiday lights. Now, 750 bulbs
send out a glow every holiday season.

Carson City's oldest tree is over 200
years old and in 1976 it was named "The
Nevada Bicentennial Tree." This cotton-
wood tree is eight feet thick!

Carson City was the crossroads for
miners and pioneers and soon it became
a fine location for a thriving trading post.
The name is taken from the Carson River,
which was named after the famous
scout, Kit Carson. Explorer John Fremont
and Carson together drew the first
map of Nevada.

Dedicate the letter **D**
to a woman called Dat-So-La-Lee.
Decorative baskets she would weave
so a history of her people she could leave.

Dat-So-La-Lee was the last of the great Washoe artists who knew the ancient art of weaving their tribal history and stories into baskets. As a child she gathered reeds and willow stems and then dyed them using tree bark and roots, later weaving them into fine baskets. She is best known for her degíkup (day-gee-coop) baskets. These baskets begin with a small base, extending to a large circle, then becoming smaller until the opening at the top is the same size as the base.

She was born about 1850 in the Carson Valley and lived to be nearly 96 years old. In her later years, when her eyesight was not as sharp as it once was, she had become so talented at weaving the intricate designs that she no longer needed to see well to create these baskets.

E

We hear "Eureka"
bringing us to E.
After digging in the rocky ground,
it was gold they came to see.

"EUREKA" could be heard during the 1800's mining boom as many people discovered gold and silver in Nevada. Some believed elf-like creatures called "tommyknockers" made tapping noises where there was gold. When there was no more "tapping," and the mines became bare, the families left for ranchlands and cities. A town named Eureka is located in the northern part of Nevada, also called "Miner Country."

Gold is still mined in Nevada and the state leads the United States in the production of gold. It is the third-highest gold producer in the world behind Australia and South Africa.

The word *eureka* means "I found it," and was first uttered by the Greek inventor Archimedes in about 225 B.C. when he found a way to measure the purity of gold.

The official colors of Nevada are blue and silver and these are both represented on our state flag. The background of the flag is blue; in the upper left-hand corner is a five-pointed silver star surrounded by sagebrush. Since the state was admitted to the Union during the Civil War, "Battle Born" is printed across the top and is a fitting slogan. Nevada was the only state to enter the Union during the Civil War years. Above the state name is a silver star representing silver, our state mineral. Nevada, a Spanish word for "snowclad," is also printed on the flag as a reminder of the towering peaks of the Sierra Nevada mountain range. The flag's design was changed a few times before its present design was adopted in 1991.

Ff

F is for our Flag a flyin'
with "Nevada" glistening gold
and shining stars of silver
to honor treasures we still hold.

Our first great seal was approved by the leaders of the Territory of Nevada on November 29, 1861. At that time the motto of the territory was "Able and Willing" and it appeared on the seal. In 1866 the state adopted a motto: "All for Our Country" which is shown on today's seal.

The 36 stars on the inner ring of the seal tell us that Nevada was the 36th state admitted to the Union in 1864. Everything on the seal has important meaning related to many interesting facts about Nevada—there is a silver miner and his team moving a carload of ore from a mountain and a quartz mill is also shown. There is a train moving across the background, lined with telegraph poles. This represents transportation and communication in Nevada. Agriculture in our state is shown by a sheaf of wheat, a sickle, and a plow. A bright sun rising over snow-capped peaks symbolizes Nevada's natural beauty.

G g

G becomes our Great state seal.
Making it look quite grand,
ranchland, lakes, and mountains tall
this seal sure tells it all!

H h

Construction of Hoover Dam began in 1930 and was completed in 1935. It was built using enough concrete to construct a two-lane highway from San Francisco to New York. Hoover Dam spans a canyon of the Colorado River. It is part of a system which provides water to more than 18 million people in the southwest United States and has 17 generators giving it the capacity to produce large amounts of electricity.

Lake Mead was created by Hoover Dam and is the largest man-made lake in the country. It has become a popular spot for water sports and fishing in Nevada. The lake also provides water for fruit, vegetables, and food for animals. Nevada produces crops such as alfalfa hay, barley, wheat, oats, and potatoes.

Hard hats, worn today for safety on construction sites, were invented to protect the workers who built Hoover Dam.

H is for Hoover Dam,
steel, strong, and might.
Gives us water and power
every day and night.

Introducing letter I and Ichthyosaurs
that lived during the time of dinosaurs.
These interesting reptiles' remains were found
on mountains considered sacred ground.

Ichthyosaur

The name, Ichthyosaur (ick-thee-oh-sor) comes from the Greek word *Ichthys*, which means "fish reptile" but they were not fish at all; they were reptiles. Ichthyosaurs bore their young alive, and were air-breathing. They lived about the same time as dinosaurs. Dr. Charles Camp discovered the fossilized remains of our ichthyosaurs in 1928 and the prehistoric reptile was declared our state fossil in 1977. Nevada is the only state that has a complete, 55-foot long skeleton of the ichthyosaur.

The Shoshones have declared the mountain where the ichthyosaurs were found to be a sacred site. The name of Nevada's ichthyosaur was changed to shonisaurus, which means reptile of the Shoshone Mountains.

I i

Velma Johnston earned the nickname "Wild Horse Annie" because of her work to save the wild horses. Born in Nevada, this noble woman saved wild horses and burros from extinction. She showed that one person can make a difference.

When "Annie" learned how cruel the wild horse roundups could be, she took action making speeches and asking children across the land to write letters to Congress and the Senate for their help in saving the wild horses.

Finally people listened. On December 15, 1971, Congress passed the Wild Free-roaming Horse and Burro Act to save animals on public lands forever. Today about 48,000 wild horses run free.

J j

Wild horses couldn't keep us away
from Velma Johnston and letter J,
a woman who worked courageously
so that horses could run free.

Have you ever lost your way
        like Nancy Kelsey, our letter K?
Her wagon train got off course
        and she had to deal with nature's force.

k
K

In 1841 Nancy Kelsey was part of the Bidwell-Bartleson wagon train. The leaders were unprepared and had no compass, directions, or maps. As they traveled over rough terrain they had to give up their wagons and supplies, including extra food and clothing. Even though she was expecting her second child, Nancy carried her young daughter much of the way. In spite of her difficulties, Nancy was the first non-Indian woman to reach California by traveling overland from the East, and she did it by going through Nevada.

Her group knew the Humboldt River existed and thought they could follow it to the Pacific Ocean. But what they didn't know is that the largest river in Nevada doesn't reach the ocean, but simply disappears into the ground in a spot called the Humboldt Sink.

Las Vegas is Spanish for "the meadows," but some like to call it the most exciting city in the whole world. One three-mile street of hotels is often called "the strip" and these enormous hotels have special decorations and entertainment. The largest hotel in Las Vegas is the MGM Grand, with over 5,000 rooms. There are other hotels with themes such as a make-believe Egyptian pyramid and the Eiffel tower.

Visitors can also watch pirate ships battle or jump aboard a double-loop roller coaster, or take in a magic show. In downtown Las Vegas we can visit museums, sample chocolates in a candy factory, ride ponies in a park, or go up in a balloon to see it all from the sky.

The Las Vegas Chamber of Commerce unveiled "Vegas Vic" in 1947—a giant, neon trimmed, cowboy-hat-wearing figure on Fremont Street in downtown Las Vegas. Vegas Vic was built to create attention for Las Vegas and the casinos. He now has a tall companion, Vegas Vicki, glittering nearby.

L is for Las Vegas, always fun—
circus, zoo, and lots of shows.
And standing 75 feet tall,
Vegas Vic welcomes all.

M m

Beatty Mudmound, that's our **M**.
It was filled with fossils galore.
Many came to dig for them
so there may not be many more.

It all happened in 1960, when geologists who were mapping around the area saw the amazing 270-foot thick, and 1,000 foot-long mound of pale gray limestone. They were excited because it proved to be the largest and best preserved of the three mudmounds in Nevada. It is named after the nearby town of Beatty. This mound is about 115 miles north of Las Vegas.

The Beatty Mudmound is famous because it contains the most complete fossil record of any 15-million-year-old deposit in the world. Many fossils at the Beatty site were buried there about 480 million years ago.

For amateur collectors and professionals the mound is a special treat, but in the near future it is likely that the government will make the extraordinary mudmound off-limits to all but scientists.

Gastropod

Trilobite

Brachiopod

GREAT BASIN

WHEELER PEAK

Great Basin National Park

LEHMAN CAVES

Great Basin National Park

N n

Great Basin National Park, in eastern Nevada, was established in 1986 and is a splendid tribute to the Great Basin region. From its sagebrush near the base to the mountaintop peaks, this park provides the perfect spot to learn much about Nevada.

Within this national park is Lehman Caves. There is just one cave, though its name may fool you. It is a beautiful cave that goes a quarter mile into marble and limestone with seemingly unlimited and unusual formations. The cave is also used to study climate changes and their effects on plants and animals.

Wheeler Peak is located in the center of the Great Basin and is the state's second highest peak. At over 13,063 feet, this mountain has a permanent ice cap and interesting glacial formations. Boundary Peak, part of the Sierra Nevada range in the western part of the state, is the highest peak in Nevada.

Have you ever been **N** to a National Park and our letter **N**?
Lakes, streams, and forests too,
it'll make quite an impression on you.

Famous for their size and shape
our precious gemstone is our O.
Black Opal—it's what we all know.
Many, many want them so.

On May 27, 1987, Nevada adopted the black opal as our state precious gemstone. The Virgin Valley is the only place in North America where such spectacular opals are found in significant quantities. Native Americans believed that if they gazed deeply into the fiery soul of the stone, they would have good luck.

Where do these precious stones come from? They are found in layers of clay formed when volcanic ash filled ancient lakes millions of years ago. Opals are fossilized bits and pieces of plants that have become "opalized." It takes nearly 10 million years to form a fiery reddish black opal.

Oo

Pp

It took millions of years to form Pyramid Lake. It is the remains of Lake Lahontan, an inland sea that covered 8,000 square miles about 11 million years ago. It is the only lake in the world that is home to the unique cui-ui fish as well as cutthroat trout and is the largest natural lake completely within Nevada. Anaho Island, located in Pyramid Lake, is one of the only American white pelican nesting sites in North America. Pyramid Lake is about 30 miles northeast of Sparks.

Also a natural lake, Lake Tahoe, with its 72 miles of shoreline, lies partly in Nevada and partly in California. At a 6,223-foot altitude, it is North America's largest mountain lake and the third deepest freshwater lake in the United States. During the winter months, visitors to Lake Tahoe can ski at Heavenly ski resort and enjoy the slopes in two states. Lake Tahoe-Nevada State Park offers sandy beaches, boat launches, picnicking, bike trails and many more warm weather activities.

Other natural lakes in Nevada are Washoe, Pahranagat, Walker, and Ruby.

Presenting Pyramid Lake for letter P.
It's what remains of an inland sea
and in its center—what a shock—
a five-hundred-foot pyramid of rock!

Q, a quantity of Quarters.
There are quite a lot
when you're very lucky
and hit a big jackpot.

Eva Adams, born in Wonder, Nevada, was named director of the United States Mint in 1961. President John F. Kennedy wanted someone who understood precious metals and the states that produced them to serve as the Mint's director.

The United States once had a mint in Carson City that ran from 1870 to 1893 because Nevada was mining so much gold and silver.

When the United States Mint was making the country's first coins, it is said that Martha Washington helped out by donating her best silver spoons. While Eva was in office, the government began making quarters in three layers— the core is copper, and the other two layers are nickel alloys.

Some might say that quarters became the most popular coin when the modern slot machine was perfected in the 1890s. It takes about 39 armored trucks two nights to deliver millions of quarters to only one of the many casinos in Las Vegas.

Qq

r R

R stands for our state Reptile.
The desert tortoise is very wise.
Hiding away from heat and cold,
so it might live to be 70 years old.

These reptiles have been around for at least one million years and have lived in the southwestern United States for the last 10,000 to 12,000 years. Desert tortoises are easy to recognize by their thick, elephant-like legs. Their front legs are larger than the rear, so that they can dig deep burrows to escape the sizzling heat and freezing cold. Vegetarians, they eat only grasses, blossoms, and cactus. These tortoises grow very slowly and breeding happens when they are 15-20 years old. Females lay four to six eggs from early May to July. In 90-120 days their white, oblong eggs will hatch into two-inch-long babies.

Near Las Vegas there is a protected area for the desert tortoise where you can study this, the largest Mojave Desert reptile.

Sagebrush, our silvery-gray state flower, has yellow blossoms, and covers 40 percent of Nevada. Even with little rain, this hardy bush keeps on growing, spreading, and blooming. Sagebrush grows everywhere in the Great Basin. One nickname for Nevada is the "The Sagebrush State."

Native Americans used sagebrush as dye, fuel, medicine, and part of religious ceremonies.

Some like to burn sagebrush in their fireplaces because it smells like spicy apple cider. When it rains, wet sagebrush has a distinctive smell. Nevada campers can enjoy sitting around a campfire smelling the spicy apple cider scent of sagebrush, and singing Nevada's state song, written by Bertha Raffetto, "Home Means Nevada."

Letter S is here to show
our state flower is able to grow
where other plants may not survive
scented Sagebrush can still thrive.

Ss

An evergreen, the single leaf pinon keeps its short, stiff needles all year, and is found growing on rocky slopes and hills. It was chosen as the Nevada state tree in 1953. The second state tree, the bristlecone pine, was chosen by Ely schoolchildren in 1987, when they discovered that some were older than the California sequoias and living in our own state.

A man named Dr. Schulman studied the bristlecone pines in the mid-1950s and thought the oldest was about 4,000 years old. But then a geology student saw a tree that appeared even older, and he bored a hole in its trunk, pulling out a core that clearly showed 4,900 rings. Unfortunately the bore broke, and the foolish young student cut the tree down to release the boring machine. He sawed off a slice of trunk showing the 4,900 rings and gave it to a restaurant to put on display. And there it is, what WAS the oldest tree in the whole world!

Some bristlecone pines are now protected in our Great Basin National Park.

Tt

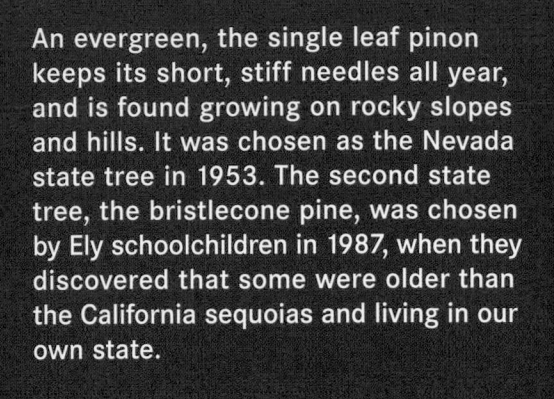

PIÑON PINE

BRISTLECONE PINE

T stands for our two state Trees—
 single leaf pinon is famous for nuts,
but bristlecone pine has it beat,
 living so long through drought and heat.

In 1874 the state university opened as a preparatory school in Elko. At this time Elko was a small railroad town just four years old. There was only money for one professor, and seven students attended. In 1885 the school in Elko was moved to Reno, nearer the state's busiest mining district, the Comstock Lode, and the state capital in Carson City, where it became a full-fledged university.

The Mackay School of Mines, world renowned for its training of mining engineers, is on the Reno campus of the University of Nevada. John Mackay made his fortune during the Comstock mining boom and his family has made many donations to the school.

An extension of the University of Nevada at Reno first held classes in Southern Nevada in an extra classroom at Las Vegas High School in 1951. At that time there was one professor and 12 students. A few years later the extension was named Nevada Southern, and in 1969 it became an independent school—the University of Nevada, Las Vegas (UNLV).

U
u

In Las Vegas or Reno,
University starts with U.
Where would you go?
There is so much you can do.

It's named Virginia City.
Let's have this become our V.
Digging through the rocky ground—
success at last, when silver and gold are found.

One of the richest silver strikes in history, found near Virginia City, was discovered by two Irish miners in 1859, but was actually named after Henry Paige Comstock. Some believe Henry did so much bragging about the lode that it was eventually called the Comstock Lode, known as the largest silver deposit in North America.

Square set timbering was invented by Philipp Deidesheimer in the Ophir Mine of Virginia City. He never sought a patent for his invention; rather, to increase safety in the mines, he let anyone use his method. Deidesheimer's invention enabled the deep mines in the area to produce many millions of bullion.

Soon, hundreds of miners brought their families and settled in Virginia City. Additional discoveries of silver and gold brought more people, making it one of the largest cities in the West at that time, except for San Francisco. The mines provided silver that helped the Union win the Civil War.

Comstock Mine

International Hotel

Mackay Mansion

Henry Paige Comstock

With **W**, a wonderful letter,
we honor someone who wanted life better.
Chief Winnemucca wished that wars would cease
so that all people could live in peace.

Chief Winnemucca

Winnemucca was chief of an Indian nation called the Paiutes. He taught his people to love peace, be kind to one another, and to respect women. It is believed that one night he dreamt that strangers with white faces would come and be his brothers. When traders visited his camp, Winnemucca shouted, "Welcome! You are the white brothers of my dream." He ordered his braves to greet visitors by riding on ponies decorated with cedar twigs and bright flowers. He helped them find the best camping places, and where to hunt for valuable skins of beavers and foxes.

When explorer John Fremont arrived, he met Chief Winnemucca's father and liked him so much that he gave him the name "Captain Truckee," which means, "all right." Until he died in 1882, Truckee helped Fremont and many other settlers.

Sarah Winnemucca

Sarah Winnemucca was born in 1844, the daughter of Chief Winnemucca. Her Paiute name, "Thocmetony," means Shell Flower. She spent her life trying to improve living conditions for her tribe. Sarah established the first school for Paiutes near Lovelock and her statue stands next to that of Sacajawea in Washington's Statuary Hall.

She was not afraid to speak to government officials in Washington, even President Rutherford B. Hayes, asking for fair treatment of her tribe. *Life Among the Piutes* was written by Sarah and it is described as a powerful legacy to her Native American culture and to the European settlers' culture. It was the first book ever published that was written by a Native American woman.

Her grandfather was Captain Truckee, who helped many newcomers to Nevada.

An extraordinary princess was so great,
X she established a school to educate.
X marks the spot where her tribe would go
to learn the things they needed to know.

Y stands for the perfect place
to enjoy life at a slower pace.
You'll relax and have some fun
in the town of Yerington.

Founded in 1878, Yerington has about 3,000 citizens who have time to leisurely sit with friends, and visitors, who soon adopt their gentle pace. Many of the families living in this agricultural community have been here for generations. Chances are in a town that is one square mile in size and without a stoplight, you're likely to pass by many folks you know.

A famous writer, Mark Twain (Samuel Clemens) spent several years in Nevada. He later wrote *Roughing It*, about his years in Nevada. Do you think he may have given his book a different title if he had been able to visit Yerington and its residents?

Wovoka was a famous Paiute mystic, who lived near Yerington, and spent his life spreading his Ghost Dance religion among many tribes across the American West. On December 19, 1975 a Wovoka historical marker was placed at the Yerington Indian Colony by the Yerington Paiute Tribe.

Z stands for Zillions of critters
scattered around our state.
You can lend a hand
for their survival upon our land.

Pronghorn
Antelope

Elko

Beaver

Reno

White Pelican

Carson City

Eureka

Western Blue
Flax

*Berlin Ichthyosaur
State Park*

*Lehman
Caves*

Mountain Lion

Black Tail Jack Rabbit

Beatty

Bald Eagle
and Lahontan a
cutthroat trout

Ash Meadows
Speckled Dace

*Valley of Fire
State Park*

Las Vegas

Henderson

Desert Tortoise

Alpine Lily

Nevada is the driest state, but there are zillions of creatures living in our deserts. What a surprise! We have 4,000 species of plants, fish, amphibians, reptiles, birds, and mammals. Our plants and animals depend on each other and the environment to survive. Many animals need plants for food, shade, and shelter. Many plants need insects, birds, and animals to spread their seeds, and pollinate their flowers. Some animals eat only certain kinds of plants, and picky eaters prefer only special parts of plants.

Our state grass, Indian Grass, grows throughout the state, looking like an untidy bunch of feathers. It is known for its ability to reseed and establish itself in areas damaged by fire or overgrazing.

Most Nevadans are careful not to harm any part of this precious state, and are proud to help visitors understand and appreciate our deserts, lakes, mountains, and rivers—and all our critters, no matter how small.

A Silver Streak of Facts

1. What does Nevada mean?

2. What is a Tommyknocker?

3. What is Nevada's state reptile?

4. What is the capital of Nevada?

5. What does the mountain bluebird, Nevada's state bird eat?

6. Why is Sarah Winnemucca famous?

7. What is Nevada's state flower?

8. Why is the motto of Nevada "Battle Born"?

9. How does much of Nevada get power and water everyday?

10. What does Las Vegas mean?

11. What is a fossil?

12. What is an artifact?

13. What tree is one of the oldest living things in the world?

14. What city was called "Queen of the West"?

15. Who was Wild Horse Annie?

16. How long can a tortoise live?

17. How can we help preserve our special environment?

Eleanor Coerr

Eleanor Coerr began her professional life as a newspaper reporter and editor of a column for children. She taught children's literature at Monterey Peninsula College and creative writing at Chapman College in California.

For the past 25 years Eleanor has been involved with writing children's books and lecturing. She has visited many schools in the United States and abroad.

Her previous children's books include *Sadako and the Thousand Paper Cranes, The Big Balloon Race, The Josefina Story Quilt, Buffalo Bill and the Pony Express,* and *Chang's Paper Pony.*

Presently Eleanor and her husband make their home in Asheville, North Carolina.

Darcie Park

Darcie started drawing when she was five or six years old, watercolor painting at seven, and she created her first oil painting at 12 years old. She started her freelance illustration career in college and illustrated her first children's book, *The Reluctant Dragon,* soon after graduating with a bachelor of fine arts degree in illustration from California State University, Long Beach.

She is a member of the CSULB alumni, the Society of Illustrators of Los Angeles, Society of Children's Book Writers and Illustrators, Sierra Nevada Artist Guild, and the Kiwanis Sunrisers.

Born and raised in Long Beach, California, Darcie now lives in an historic cabin in Lake Tahoe.

Answers

1. It is the Spanish work for snow-capped.

2. An imaginary elf who helped miners find gold

3. A desert tortoise

4. Carson City

5. Seeds, berries, fruit, and insects

6. She worked hard to help the Paiute tribe

7. Sagebrush

8. Because our state was admitted to the Union during the Civil War.

9. From Hoover Dam

10. It is Spanish for "the meadows."

11. A fossil is the entombed remains of many species of extinct animals and plants.

12. An artifact is something made by hand millions of years ago.

13. Bristlecone pine, one of Nevada's state trees

14. Virginia City

15. Velma Johnston, who protected wild horses

16. About 70 years

17. Respect the desert and drive on roads. Don't leave trash. Be careful not to hurt plants or animals. Can you think of other ways?